SIGNS OF THE SEASONS

Signs of Winter

Paul Humphrey

Photography by Chris Fairclough

W

FRANKLIN WATTS
LONDON•SYDNEY

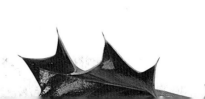

© 2001 Franklin Watts

First published in Great Britain by
Franklin Watts
96 Leonard Street
London
EC2A 4XD

Franklin Watts Australia
56 O'Riordan Street
Alexandria
NSW 2015

ISBN: 0 7496 4039 1
Dewey Decimal Classification 574.5
A CIP catalogue record for this book is available from the British Library

Printed in Hong Kong/China

Planning and production by Discovery Books
Editors: Tamsin Osler, Kate Banham
Design: Ian Winton
Art Direction: Jason Anscomb

Photographs:
Bruce Coleman: 15 (John Cancalosi), 16 (Janos Jurka);
Corbis: 9 (Karen Huntt Mason); Linpac Environmental: 25;
Oxford Scientific Films: 24 (Anna Walsh); PhotoDisc 29 (PhotoLink);
Tony Stone Images: 20 (Timothy Shonnard), 22 (Philip and Karen Smith).
All other photography by Chris Fairclough.

'When All the World Is Full of Snow' from *Hurry, Hurry, Mary Dear!*
and Other Nonsense Poems © 1976 N.M. Bodecker.
Reproduced by kind permission of the publishers, J.M. Dent & Sons Ltd.

CONTENTS

Winter is here. Look for the signs of winter.

It is still dark when you wake up in the morning.

It's cold outside. Sometimes there is frost on the ground and on leaves and branches.

The windows on Mum's car are frosty, too.

When it's very cold, icicles form
and hang from the roof and gutters.

You have to wear a warm winter coat...

...and a scarf, hat and gloves.

You can see your own breath.

Your fingers and toes feel cold.

The branches on most trees are bare.

It is hard for the birds
to find food and
water.

Some birds feed on winter berries.

You can put nuts and seeds
in the bird feeder.

The farmer brings the cows into
the warm barn.

He ploughs the fields ready for planting in the spring.

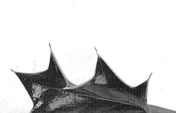

Sometimes it is very wet in winter.

You have to spend more time indoors.

If you're lucky it snows, and you can
build a snowman...

...or go sledging.

The snowplough clears the snow.

Salt and grit on the road melts
the snow and ice.

Winter evenings are dark and cold.
You turn on the central heating...

...or light a fire, and are happy to stay warm indoors.

What other signs of winter can you see?

When All the World Is Full of Snow

I never know
just where to go,
when all the world
is full of snow.

I do not want
to make a track,
not even
to the shed and back.

I only want
to watch and wait,
while snow moths settle
on the gate,

and swarming frost flakes
fill the trees
with billions
of albino bees.

I only want
myself to be
as silent as
a winter tree,

to hear the swirling
stillness grow,
when all the world
is full of snow.

N. M. Bodecker

INDEX